INSECURITY

FEELING OF NOT MEASURING UP TO SOCIETY'S STANDARDS

A COMPARATIVE STUDY

Sandipkumar Navneetbhai Patel
Adhoc Lecturer,
Department of Psychology,
Nalini Arvind and T.V. Patel Arts College
Sardar Patel University, Vallabh Vidyanagar
Gujarat (India)

Publish World

2015

Price : $27.86

First Edition : 2015

ISBN : 978-1-926488-06-6

ISBN Allotment Agency : Library and Archives Canada (Govt. of Canada)

Published & Printed by
Canadian Academic Publishing
81, Woodlot Crescent,
Etobicoke,
Toronto, Ontario, Canada.
Postal Code- M9W 6T3
Phone- +1 (647) 633 9712
http://www.canadapublish.com

FORWARD

Insecurity is a lack of self-worth, a doubt and uncertainty, and feeling of not measuring up to society's standards. It is often subconscious, and is thought to drive afflicted individuals to overcompensate, resulting either in spectacular achievement or extreme antisocial behaviour. The term was coined to indicate a lack of covert self esteem.

Insecurity"is a book of psychology measuring the insecurity in men and woman of higher and lower status. This book of psychology will give the inspirational guidance to the students in their future. Patel Sandipkumar N has achieved M.A and M.Phil degree in Postgraduate section of Psychology from Sardar Patel University. Currently, he is working on Ph.D degree. He is peculiar and fascinated in research. His more than ten (10) research papers are published in several journals. He has delightful proficiency of writing books from childhood.

Dr. M.G.Mansuri
Associate Prof. and Head
Department of Psychology
Nalini Arvind and T.V. Patel Arts College
Sardar Patel University, Vallabh Vidyanagar

ACKNOWLEDGEMENT

I am thankful to Nalini, Arvind & T. V. Patel Arts College for providing me Adhoc Lecturarship and encouragment during the book writing. I also thank Dr. L. R. Yagnik, Department of Psychology, Sardar Patel University and Dr. M. G. Mansuri, Associate Professor, Department of Psychology, Nalini, Arvind & T. V. Patel Arts College, Sardar Patel University. I extend my thank to all experimental model for their kind co-operation.

- **Sandipkumar Navneetbhai Patel**
Adhoc Lecturer, Department of Psychology
Nalini, Arvind and T.V. Patel Arts College
Vallabh Vidyanagar, Gujarat (India)

CONTENTS

I. GENERAL INTRODUCTION

WHAT IS INSECURITY ?

Insecurity is a lack of self-worth, a doubt and uncertainty, and feeling of not measuring up to society's standards. It is often subconscious, and is thought to drive afflicted individuals to overcompensate, resulting either in spectacular achievement or extreme antisocial behaviour. The term was coined to indicate a lack of covert self esteem. For many, it is developed through a combination of genetic personality characteristics and personal experiences.

Research on the psychological consequences of Insecurity is reviewed, showing that insecurity reduces psychological well-being and satisfaction, and increases psychosomatic complaints and physical strains. Next, three additional research questions are addressed, since these questions did not receive much attention in previous research.

CLASSIFICATION

Classical Adlerian psychology makes a distinction between primary and secondary inferiority feelings.

- A primary inferiority feeling is said to be rooted in the young child's original experience of weakness, helplessness and dependency. It can then be intensified by comparisons to siblings, romantic partners, and adults.
- A secondary inferiority feeling relates to an adult's experience of being unable to reach a subconscious, fictional final goal of subjective

1

security and success to compensate for the inferiority feelings. The perceived distance from that goal would lead to a negative/depressed feeling that could then prompt the recall of the original inferiority feeling; this composite of inferiority feelings could be experienced as overwhelming. The goal invented to relieve the original, primary feeling of inferiority which actually causes the secondary feeling of inferiority is the "catch-22" of this dilemma. This vicious circle is common in neurotic lifestyles.

Feeling insecure is often viewed as being inferior to another person, but this is not always the case in the Adlerian view. One often feels incompetent to perform a task, such as a test in school.

According to general psychology Insecurity is divided in main Eight sub-classess.

1. Future Context Insecurity
2. Study Context Insecurity
3. Survival Context Insecurity
4. Family Context Insecurity
5. Self Context Insecurity
6. Peer Group Context Insecurity
7. School Context Insecurity
8. Exam Context Insecurity

CAUSES

Insecurity occurs when the feelings of inferiority are intensified in the individual through discouragement or failure. Those who are at risk for developing a complex include people who: show signs of low self-esteem or self-worth, are of different ethnicity, have low socioeconomic status, or have a history of depression symptoms. Children reared in households who were constantly criticized or did not live up to parents expectations may also develop this. Many times there are warning signs to someone who may be more prone to developing Insecurity. For example, someone who is prone to attention and approval seeking behaviours may be more susceptible. Often, it is difficult to place an exact cause to the development of Insecurity. Race, gender, sexual orientation, social class, mental health, physical appearance, or any character that is not within society's normative dominant traits can contribute to this.

MANIFESTATIONS

When Insecurity is in full effect, it may impact the performance of the individual as well as impact the individual's self-esteem. Unconscious psychological and emotional processes can disrupt students' cognitive learning, and negatively "charged" feeling-toned memory associations can derail the learning process. Hutt found that math can become associated with a psychological Insecurity, low motivation and self-efficacy, poor self-directed learning strategies, and feeling unsafe or anxious.

Widely researched, but often not talked about specifically in this area is the concept of self-esteem and that people can feel good about their abilities and have self-esteem in areas where they feel competent and might not hold such personal esteem in other areas of their life. In essence, self-esteem can also be context-driven. Thus, the theory that someone has an overarching Insecurity is a bit outdated.

In the mental health treatment population, this characteristic is shown in patients with many disorders such as certain types of schizophrenia, mood disorders, and personality disorders. Moritz found the people suffering from paranoid schizophrenia used their delusions as a defense mechanism against low implicit self esteem.

Present Book represents a comparative study of 'Insecurity' in upper and lower class youth. The all eight sub-classes – Future context Insecurity, Study context Insecurity, Survival context Insecurity, Family context Insecurity, Self context Insecurity, Peer Group context Insecurity context Insecurity, School context Insecurity, Exam context Insecurity are studied extensively. Here we have chosen 18 to 35 years old fellows in both upper and lower class category. Insecurity measurement was carried out by using 'Scale of Insecurity' created by Dr. Beena Shah. After statistical analysis of all data, we found vast different in degree of Insecurity between Upper and lower class youth. We have studied Self context Insecurity by taking three independent variables using F-Anova test with 2x2x2 factorial design.

II. PAST STUDIES IN INSECURITY

STUDY-1

Title: 'Impact of attributional style and gender difference on insecurity feeling'

Researcherer: Gnufran M. (2006). Kumaun University, Uttaranchal

Aim of Study: The aim of this study was to analyze the INSECURITY in context of Age, Caste and characters

Sample: Total 240 samples were selected, of which 120 external and 120 internal controls

Tools: (1) Locus of control scale, Kumar and Shrivastav (1985)

      (2) Insecurity Inventory, Shrivastav (1976)

Statistical analysis:

Present study was done by 2x2x2 method and data analysis was done by F-test

Conclusion:
1.   Insecurity with respect to age shows significant difference

2.   Insecurity with respect to caste doesn't show any significant difference

3.   Insecurity with respect to character doesn't show any significant difference

STUDY-2

Title: 'Study of INSECURITY in employee of Government and National bank'

Researcherer: Master of Arts students (2003), Sardar Patel University

Aim of Study: The aim of this study was to analyze the INSECURITY in bank employee with reference to type of bank, caste and work experience

Sample: Total 240 samples were selected, from different bank

Tools: INSECURITY measuring tool having 70 sentences

Statistical analysis:

Present study was done by 2x2x2 method and data analysis was done by F-test

Conclusion:

1.   Insecurity with respect to Government and non government bank shows significant difference

2.   Insecurity with respect to sex doesn't show any significant difference

3.   Insecurity with respect to work experience doesn't show any significant difference

STUDY-3

Title: 'Study of INSECURITY and Adjustment in Joint and disperse family students'

Aim of Study: The aim of this study was to analyze INSECURITY and Adjustment in Joint and disperse family students'

Sample: Total 320 samples were selected

Tools: (1) INSECURITY measuring tool, Dr. Beena Shah

       (2) Bell Adjustment Sanshodhanica, Dr. Bell

Statistical analysis:

Present study was done by 2x2x2 method and data analysis was done by F-test

Conclusion:
1.   Insecurity with respect residence shows significant difference

2.   Insecurity with respect to caste doesn't show any significant difference

3.   Insecurity with respect to family type doesn't show any significant difference

STUDY-4

Title: 'Study of insecurity, stress and Depression in upper and lower class youth'

Researcher: Mr. Sandip N. Patel (2010), Sardar Patel University

Aim of Study: The aim of this study was to study of insecurity, stress and Depression in upper and lower class youth.

Sample: Total 240 samples were selected, from different bank

Tools: (1) INSECURITY measuring tool, Dr. Beena Shah

       (2) Depression measuring tool, Dr. A. T. Bak (1969)

       (3) Stress measuring tool, Akther and Vadra (1998)

Statistical analysis:

Present study was done by 2x2x2 method and data analysis was done by F-test

Conclusion:
1.   Insecurity with respect to upper and lower class youth shows significant difference

2.   Insecurity with respect to rural and urban area doesn't show any significant difference

3.   Insecurity with respect to sex shows significant difference

STUDY-5

Title: 'A study of occupational stress, insecurity and work involvement among the first class industrial supervisors'

Researcher: A. P. Singh (1984)

Sample: 150 first class industrial supervisors from spinning mill.

Tools: (1) Occupational stress measuring tool,

(2) Insecurity measuring tool, Ansari (1964)

(3) Work involvement measuring tool, Kapur and Singh (1978)

Statistical analysis:

Present study was done by 2x2x2 method and data analysis was done by F-test

Conclusion:

1.   There is negative correlation between Insecurity and occupational stress.

2.   Insecurity influences the work involvement of supervisors.

3.   Occupational stress influences the work involvement of supervisors.

STUDY-6

Title: 'A study of anxiety, emotional maturity and insecurity among teenagers of single sex school'

Aim of Study: To study anxiety, emotional maturity and insecurity in teenagers of single sex school

Researcher: Charu Vyas

Sample: Students were selected from 'Majrut nagar school' industrial supervisors from spinning mill.

Conclusion: There is no significant difference in the degree of anxiety, emotional maturity and insecurity.

STUDY-7

Title: 'A study of Insecurity in student taking narcotic drugs on regular bases.'

Aim of Study: To study Insecurity in student taking narcotic drugs on regular bases

Researcher: Ravi Gujarati and Amisha Jani

Conclusion: Insecurity is significantly higher in the group taking narcotic drugs than that in group does take narcotic drugs.

STUDY-8

Gilbert and Wambert (1967) studied and concluded that personal characteristic like Anxiety, Depression cause the insecurity in different individuals. And these people generally use to take the narcotic drugs and other such thing regularly.

STUDY-9

Robinson (1949) said that the person read more and seriously are generally feels more insecure than others. They also scare than normal individuals. They also have characteristics like short temperament, shy and less concentrative.

III. FUTURE CONTEXT INSECURITY

COMPARISON BETWEEN HIGHER AND LOWER CLASS YOUTH

"Man is social animal"- this is very old and true saying, describes relationship between man and their surrounding social components\environment. Man strikes with many state of mind during their whole life while interacting with social components. One such state of mind is Inferiority complex. When man does not get social and emotional support from his family as well as from social environment, gradually he develops Inferiority complex in his mind. And this Inferiority complex gradually develops in to 'Insecurity'. Insecurity means "The Inferiority complex created due to the external factors/catalysis of surrounding environment". There are main three types of Insecurity: Social Insecurity, Psychological Insecurity and Ecological Insecurity. Here we try to measure the degree of Insecurity in higher and lower class youth. We mainly focused our study on mainly three components of Insecurity which are Family context Insecurity, Future context Insecurity and Existence context Insecurity (Raja, 1982).

OBJECTIVES

- To measure degree of Insecurity in higher and lower class youth
- To compare degree of Insecurity between higher and lower class youth

RESEARCH METHODOLOGY

(Dhila, 2004; Shah, 1989)

- Independent Variables

A = Economical Status A_1 = Higher class (Annual income > 20,000 rupees)

A_2 = Lower class(Annual income $\leq$ 20,000 rupees)

B = Area\Location B_1 = City (Town)

B_2 = Rural

C = Sex C_1 = Boys

C_2 = Girl

- Dependent Variables

Degree of Future context Insecurity

HYPOTHESIS

Ho_1 : There is no significant difference between Means(M) of the degree of future context Insecurity between higher and lower class youth.

Ho_2 : There is no significant difference between Means(M) of the degree of future context Insecurity between city and rural area youth.

Ho_3 : There is no significant difference between Means(M) of the degree of future context Insecurity between boys and girls.

TOOLS

- Personal information sheet
- Insecurity measurement scale (Dr. Beena Shah)
- Statistical analysis of data by F-Anova test using 2x2x2 factorial design

SAMPLE

Total 240 youngsters were selected. Out of 240, 120 were of higher class and 120 were of lower class. Out of these 120, 60 were from city/town area and 60 were from rural area. Sex ratio was maintained 1:1 in these sample of 60. It means out of these 60, 30 were boys and 3o were girls.

STATISTICAL ANALYSIS

(Parekh and Dixit, 1995)

Table -1

Summary of the 2x2x2 analysis of variance based on degree of future context Insecurity with respect to three independent variables

Score of Variable	Sum of Square	DF	Mean of Square	F	Sig.
Status (A)	244.017	1	244.017	23.035	0.01
Aria (B)	8.817	1	8.817	8.32	0.05
Sex (C)	84.017	1	84.017	7.93	0.05
A x B	3.267	1	3.267	3.08	N.S.
B x C	6.667	1	6.667	6.29	0.05
A x C	68.267	1	68.267	6.45	0.05
A x B x C	6.017	1	6.017	5.68	N.S.

Table -2

Mean Scores and difference of Mean degree of future context Insecurity with respect to three independent variables

Independent Variables		N	Mean(M)	Difference Of Mean
Status (A)	Higher	120	8.23	2.02
	Lower	120	6.21	
Aria (B)	City(Town)	120	7.03	0.38
	Rural	120	7.41	
Sex (C)	Boys	120	6.63	1.18
	Girls	120	7.81	

RESULTS AND DISCUSSION

Ho_1 : There is no significant difference between Means(M) of the degree of future context Insecurity between higher and lower class youth.

The 'F – Value' for first set of independent variable was found 23.035 as shown in table-1. This result has 0.01 significance value. So above said hypothesis Ho_1 cannot be accepted because result has significant difference. Thus statistical data of table-1 clearly shown that there is significant difference in the degrees of future context Insecurity between higher and lower class youth. Mean values for higher and lower class were 8.23 and 6.21 respectively (Table-2). These mean values concluded that the degree of future context Insecurity is significantly higher in higher class than that of lower class.

Ho$_2$: There is no significant difference between Means(M) of the degree of future context Insecurity between city and rural area youth.

The 'F – Value' for second set of independent variable was found 8.32 as shown in table-1. This result has 0.05 significance value. So above said hypothesis **Ho$_2$** cannot be accepted because result has significant difference. Thus statistical data of table-1 clearly shown that there is significant difference in the degrees of future context Insecurity between city and rural area youth. Mean values for city and rural area were 7.03 and 7.41 respectively (Table-2). These mean values concluded that the degree of future context Insecurity is significantly higher in rural area than that city area youth.

Ho$_3$: There is no significant difference between Means(M) of the degree of future context Insecurity between boys and girls.

The 'F – Value' for first independent variable was found 7.93 as shown in table-1. This result has 0.05 significance value. So above said hypothesis **Ho$_3$** cannot be accepted because result has significant difference. Thus statistical data of table-1 clearly shown that there is significant difference in the degrees of future context Insecurity between boys and girls. Mean values for higher and lower class were 6.63 and 7.81 respectively (Table-2). These mean values concluded that the degree of future context Insecurity is significantly higher in girls that that in boys.

CONCLUSION

Finally we can conclude this study in following three conclusions:

- Future context Insecurity is significantly higher in higher class than that of lower class.
- Future context Insecurity is significantly higher in rural area than that city area youth.
- Future context Insecurity is significantly higher in girls that that in boys.

IV.   STUDY CONTEXT INSECURITY

COMPARISON BETWEEN HIGHER AND LOWER CLASS YOUTH

The word 'SCHOOL' is derived from Greek word 'SCHOLA'. 'SCHOLA' means sort of meeting where people get together and discuss on some pre-decided topics. The interaction of thoughts of different types of mind was occurred. Such types of interaction were cause deposition of either inferiority or superiority complexes in people's mind. It is categorized as man verses man interaction. It is inferiority complex created by biotic factor. When man does not satisfy his basic requirements during study, he gradually develops Inferiority complex in his mind. And this Inferiority complex gradually develops in to 'Insecurity'. Insecurity means "The Inferiority complex created due to the external factors/catalysis of surrounding environment". There are main three types of Insecurity: Social Insecurity, Psychological Insecurity and Ecological Insecurity. Here we try to measure the degree of Insecurity in higher and lower class youth. We mainly focused our study on 'Study context Insecurity' (Raja, 1982).

OBJECTIVES

- To measure degree of Study context Insecurity in upper and lower class youth
- To compare degree of Study context Insecurity between upper and lower class youth

RESEARCH METHODOLOGY

(Dhila, 2004; Shah, 1989)

- Independent Variables

A = Economical Status $\qquad$ A_1 = Higher class (Annual income $>$ 20,000 rupees)

A_2 = Lower class(Annual income $\leq$ 20,000 rupees)

B = Area\Location $\qquad$ B_1 = City (Town)

B_2 = Rural

C = Sex $\qquad$ C_1 = Boys

C_2 = Girl

- Dependent Variables

Degree of Study context Insecurity

HYPOTHESIS

Ho_1 : There is no significant difference between Means(M) of the degree of Study context Insecurity between Upper and lower class youth.

Ho_2 : There is no significant difference between Means(M) of the degree of Study context Insecurity between city and rural area youth.

Ho_3 : There is no significant difference between Means(M) of the degree of Study context Insecurity between boys and girls.

TOOLS

- Personal information sheet
- Insecurity measurement scale (Dr. Beena Shah)
- Statistical analysis of data by F-Anova test using 2x2x2 factorial design

SAMPLE

Total 240 youngsters were selected. Out of 240, 120 were of Upper class and 120 were of lower class. Out of these 120, 60 were from city/town area and 60 were from rural area. Sex ratio was maintained 1:1 in this sample of 60. It means out of these 60, 30 were boys and 30 were girls.

STATISTICAL ANALYSIS

(Parekh and Dixit, 1995)

Table -1

Summary of the 2x2x2 analysis of variance based on degree of Study context Insecurity with respect to three independent variables

Score of Variable	Sum of Square	DF	Mean of Square	F	Sig.
Status (A)	160.07	1	160.07	13.25	0.01
Aria (B)	3.27	1	3.27	2.70	0.01
Sex (C)	15.00	1	15.00	1.24	N.S.
A x B	1.35	1	1.35	1.12	N.S.
B x C	36.81	1	36.81	3.04	N.S.
A x C	46.40	1	46.40	3.85	N.S.
A x B x C	86.40	1	86.40	7.12	0.01

Table -2

Mean Scores and difference of Mean degree of Study context Insecurity with respect to three independent variables

Independent Variables		N	Mean(M)	Difference Of Mean
Status (A)	Upper	120	70.09	1.63
	Lower	120	5.46	
Aria (B)	City(Town)	120	6.16	0.24
	Rural	120	6.40	
Sex (C)	Boys	120	6.03	0.5
	Girls	120	6.53	

RESULTS AND DISCUSSION

Ho_1 : There is no significant difference between Means(M) of the degree of Study context Insecurity between Upper and lower class youth.

The 'F – Value' for first set of independent variable was found 13.25 as shown in table-1. This result has 0.01 significance value. So above said hypothesis **Ho_1** can not be accepted because result has significant difference. Thus statistical data of table-1 clearly shown that there is significant difference in the degrees of Study context Insecurity between Upper and lower class youth. Mean values for Upper and lower class were 7.09 and 5.46 respectively (Table-2). These mean values concluded that the degree of Study context Insecurity is significantly higher in upper class than that in lower class youth.

Ho$_2$: There is no significant difference between Means(M) of the degree of Study context Insecurity between city and rural area youth.

The 'F – Value' for second set of independent variable was found 2.70 as shown in table-1. This result has 0.01 significance value. So above said hypothesis **Ho$_2$** can not be accepted because result has significant difference. Thus statistical data of table-1 clearly shown that there is significant difference in the degrees of Study context Insecurity between city and rural area youth. Mean values for city and rural area were 6.16 and 6.40 respectively (Table-2). These mean values concluded that the degree of Study context Insecurity is significantly higher in rural area than that city area youth.

Ho$_3$: There is no significant difference between Means(M) of the degree of Study context Insecurity between boys and girls.

The 'F – Value' for first independent variable was found 1.24 as shown in table-1. This result has insignificance value. So above said hypothesis **Ho$_3$** can be accepted because result has significant difference. Thus statistical data of table-1 clearly shown that there is insignificant difference in the degrees of Study context Insecurity between boys and girls. Mean values for Upper and lower class were 6.03 and 6.53 respectively (Table-2). These mean values concluded that the difference in degree of Study context Insecurity is insignificant between girls and boys.

CONCLUSION

Finally we can conclude this study in following three conclusions:

- Study context Insecurity is significantly higher in upper class than that of lower class.
- Study context Insecurity is significantly higher in rural area than that city area youth.
- Study context Insecurity is insignificant between girls and boys.

V. SURVIVAL CONTEXT INSECURITY
COMPARISON BETWEEN HIGHER AND LOWER CLASS YOUTH

"SURVIVAL OF THE FITEST"- this is very popular principle of Charls Darwin. It describes interaction between man and man as well as men and nature. Man strikes with many hurdles during their whole life while interacting with biotic and abiotic components of his surroundings. Due to these types of interaction, he faces many state of his own mind. One of these state is Inferiority complex. When man does not get his basic requirements, he gradually develops Inferiority complex in his mind. And this Inferiority complex gradually develops in to 'Insecurity'. Insecurity means "The Inferiority complex created due to the external factors/catalysis of surrounding environment". There are main three types of Insecurity: Social Insecurity, Psychological Insecurity and Ecological Insecurity. Here we try to measure the degree of Insecurity in higher and lower class youth. We mainly focused our study on mainly three components of Insecurity which are Survival context Insecurity, Survival context Insecurity (Raja, 1982).

OBJECTIVES
- To measure degree of Survival context Insecurity in upper and lower class youth
- To compare degree of Survival context Insecurity between upper and lower class youth

RESEARCH METHODOLOGY
(Dhila, 2004; Shah, 1989)
- Independent Variables

A = Economical Status	A_1 = Upper class (Annual income $>$ 20,000 rupees)
	A_2 = Lower class(Annual income $\leq$ 20,000 rupees)
B = Area\Location	B_1 = City (Town)
	B_2 = Rural
C = Sex	C_1 = Boys
	C_2 = Girl

- Dependent Variables

Degree of Survival context Insecurity

HYPOTHESIS

Ho_1 : There is no significant difference between Means(M) of the degree of Survival context Insecurity between Upper and lower class youth.

Ho_2 : There is no significant difference between Means(M) of the degree of Survival context Insecurity between city and rural area youth.

Ho_3 : There is no significant difference between Means(M) of the degree of Survival context Insecurity between boys and girls.

TOOLS

- Personal information sheet
- Insecurity measurement scale (Dr. Beena Shah)
- Statistical analysis of data by F-Anova test using 2x2x2 factorial design

SAMPLE

Total 240 youngsters were selected. Out of 240, 120 were of Upper class and 120 were of lower-class. Out of these 120, 60 were from city/town area and 60 were from rural area. Sex ratio was maintained 1:1 in this sample of 60. It means out of these 60, 30 were boys and 30 were girls.

STATISTICAL ANALYSIS

(Parekh and Dixit, 1995)

Table -1

Summary of the 2x2x2 analysis of variance based on degree of survival context Insecurity with respect to three independent variables

Score of Variable	Sum of Square	DF	Mean of Square	F	Sig.
Status (A)	37.90	1	37..90	2.57	0.05
Aria (B)	36.23	1	36.23	2.51	0.05
Sex (C)	56.35	1	56.35	3.91	0.05
A x B	2.50	1	2.50	1.74	N.S.
B x C	37.09	1	37.09	2.57	N.S.
A x C	8.57	1	8.57	5.95	N.S.
A x B x C	133.59	1	133.59	9.27	0.05

Table -2

Mean Scores and difference of Mean degree of Survival survival Insecurity with respect to three independent variables

Independent Variables		N	Mean(M)	Difference Of Mean
Status (A)	Upper	120	6.86	0.75
	Lower	120	6.11	
Aria (B)	City(Town)	120	6.08	0.81
	Rural	120	6.89	
Sex (C)	Boys	120	6.01	0.94
	Girls	120	6.95	

RESULTS AND DISCUSSION

Ho_1 : **There is no significant difference between Means(M) of the degree of survival context Insecurity between Upper and lower class youth.**

The 'F – Value' for first set of independent variable was found 2.57 as shown in table-1. This result has 0.05 significance value. So above said hypothesis Ho_1 can not be accepted because result has significant difference. Thus statistical data of table-1 clearly shown that there is significant difference in the degrees of Survival context Insecurity between Upper and lower class youth. Mean values for Upper and lower class were 6.86 and 6.11 respectively (Table-2). These mean values concluded that the degree of Survival context Insecurity is significantly higher in upper class than that in lower class youth.

Ho$_2$: There is no significant difference between Means(M) of the degree of Survival context Insecurity between city and rural area youth.

The 'F – Value' for second set of independent variable was found 2.51 as shown in table-1. This result has 0.05 significance value. So above said hypothesis **Ho$_2$** can not be accepted because result has significant difference. Thus statistical data of table-1 clearly shown that there is significant difference in the degrees of Survival context Insecurity between city and rural area youth. Mean values for city and rural area were 6.08 and 6.89 respectively (Table-2). These mean values concluded that the degree of Survival context Insecurity is significantly higher in rural area than that city area youth.

Ho$_3$: There is no significant difference between Means(M) of the degree of Survival context Insecurity between boys and girls.

The 'F – Value' for first independent variable was found 3.31 as shown in table-1. This result has 0.05 significance value. So above said hypothesis **Ho$_3$** can not be accepted because result has significant difference. Thus statistical data of table-1 clearly shown that there is significant difference in the degrees of Survival context Insecurity between boys and girls. Mean values for Upper and lower class were 6.1 and 6.95 respectively (Table-2). These mean values concluded that the degree of Survival context Insecurity is significantly higher in girls that that in boys.

CONCLUSION

Finally we can conclude this study in following three conclusions:

- Survival context Insecurity is significantly higher in upper class than that of lower class.
- Survival context Insecurity is significantly higher in rural area than that city area youth.
- Survival context Insecurity is significantly higher in girls that that in boys.

VI. FAMILY CONTEXT INSECURITY
COMPARISON BETWEEN HIGHER AND LOWER CLASS YOUTH

'Man should live in group having some relation with one another'- above stated sentence was the dream of saint *'Manu'*. He had done many efforts to established manners and family system in life style of old ancient man, we called him *'Adi-manav'*. Then after man started to live in group and was known as *'Family'*. With the array of time family system developed more and more and today's well mannered family system is consequence of the same. But everything has two sides like coin, one is positive side and another is negative side. As 'family system' grows up, it also develops some negative impact on man's mind. The Inferiority complex created due to the family system is classified as 'Family context Insecurity'. Here we try to measure the degree of Family Context Insecurity by taking three different variables (Raja, 1982). The comparative account of the same is also discussed here by taking 'Scale of Insecurity' described by Dr. Beena Shah as a survey tool.

OBJECTIVES

- To measure degree of Family context Insecurity in upper and lower class youth
- To compare degree of Family context Insecurity between upper and lower class youth

RESEARCH METHODOLOGY

(Dhila, 2004; Shah, 1989)

- Independent Variables

A = Economical Status A_1 = Upper class (Annual income > 20,000 rupees)

A_2 = Lower class (Annual income $\leq$ 20,000 rupees)

B = Area\Location B_1 = City (Town)

B_2 = Rural

C = Sex C_1 = Boys

C_2 = Girl

- Dependent Variables

Degree of Family context Insecurity

HYPOTHESIS

Ho_1 : There is no significant difference between Means(M) of the degree of Family context Insecurity between Upper and lower class youth.

Ho_2 : There is no significant difference between Means(M) of the degree of Family context Insecurity between city and rural area youth.

Ho_3 : There is no significant difference between Means(M) of the degree of Family context Insecurity between boys and girls.

TOOLS

- Personal information sheet
- Insecurity measurement scale (Dr. Beena Shah)
- Statistical analysis of data by F-Anova test using 2x2x2 factorial design

SAMPLE

Total 240 youngsters were selected. Out of 240, 120 were of Upper class and 120 were of lowerclass. Out of these 120, 60 were from city/town area and 60 were from rural area. Sex ratio was maintained 1:1 in this sample of 60. It means out of these 60, 30 were boys and 30 were girls.

STATISTICAL ANALYSIS

(Parekh and Dixit, 1995)

Table -1

Summary of the 2x2x2 analysis of variance based on degree of Family context Insecurity with respect to three independent variables

Score of Variable	Sum of Square	DF	Mean of Square	F	Sig.
Status (A)	1316.017	1	1316.017	98.04	0.01
Aria (B)	32.267	1	32.267	2.40	N.S.
Sex (C)	123.267	1	123.267	9.18	0.05
A x B	216.600	1	216.600	16.14	0.01
B x C	308.267	1	308.267	22.97	N.S.
A x C	14.017	1	14.017	1.05	N.S.
A x B x C	84.017	1	84.017	6.26	0.05

Table -2

Mean Scores and difference of Mean degree of Family Context Insecurity with respect to three independent variables

Independent Variables		N	Mean(M)	Difference Of Mean
Status (A)	Upper	120	13.67	4.74
	Lower	120	8.93	
Aria (B)	City(Town)	120	11.69	0.73
	Rural	120	10.96	
Sex (C)	Boys	120	10.61	1.43
	Girls	120	12.04	

RESULTS AND DISCUSSION

Ho₁ : There is no significant difference between Means(M) of the degree of Family context Insecurity between Upper and lower class youth.

The 'F – Value' for first set of independent variable was found 98.04 as shown in table-1. This result has 0.01 significance value. So above said hypothesis **Ho₁** cannot be accepted because result has significant difference. Thus statistical data of table-1 clearly shown that there is significant difference in the degrees of Family context Insecurity between Upper and lower class youth. Mean values for Upper and lower class were 13.69 and 8.93 respectively (Table-2). These mean values concluded that the degree of Family context Insecurity is significantly higher in upper class than that in lower class youth.

Ho₂ : There is no significant difference between Means(M) of the degree of Family context Insecurity between city and rural area youth.

The 'F – Value' for second set of independent variable was found 2.40 as shown in table-1. This result has no significance value. So above said hypothesis **Ho₂** can be accepted because result has significant difference. Thus statistical data of table-1 clearly shown that there is significant difference in the degrees of Family context Insecurity between city and rural area youth. Mean values for city and rural area were 11.69 and 10.96 respectively (Table-2). These mean values concluded that the degree of Family context Insecurity is insignificantly differing between rural area and city area youth.

Ho₃ : There is no significant difference between Means(M) of the degree of Family context Insecurity between boys and girls.

The 'F – Value' for first independent variable was found 9.18 as shown in table-1. This result has 0.05 significance value. So above said hypothesis **Ho₃** cannot be accepted because result has significant difference. Thus statistical data of table-1 clearly shown that there is significant difference in the degrees of Family context Insecurity between boys and girls. Mean values for Upper and lower class were 10.61 and 12.04 respectively (Table-2). These mean values concluded that the degree of Family context Insecurity is significantly higher in girls that that in boys.

CONCLUSION

Finally we can conclude this study in following three conclusions:

- Family context Insecurity is significantly higher in upper class than that of lower class.
- Family context Insecurity is insignificantly differs between rural area and city area youth.
- Family context Insecurity is significantly higher in girls that that in boys.

VII. SELF CONTEXT INSECURITY
COMPARISON BETWEEN HIGHER AND LOWER CLASS YOUTH

Man likes to live in group, and this is believed to be one of the major factors that affect the psychological feathers man develops during his life regarding the 'Insecurity'. Man interacts with man by many ways during his whole life and strikes with many hurdles while interacting with such biotic factors. He faces many state of his own mind. One of these state is Inferiority complex. When man does not get his basic requirements, he gradually develops Inferiority complex in his mind. And this Inferiority complex gradually develops in to 'Insecurity'. Insecurity means "The Inferiority complex created due to the external factors/catalysis of surrounding environment". Moreover Dr Sigmund Freund said that man suffered by inferiority complex with rather higher intensity in groups. Here we try to measure the degree of Self-context Insecurity by taking three independent variables in account (Raja, 1982).

OBJECTIVES
- To measure degree of Self context Insecurity in upper and lower class youth
- To compare degree of Self context Insecurity between upper and lower class youth

RESEARCH METHODOLOGY

(Dhila, 2004; Shah, 1989)

- Independent Variables

A = Economical Status	A_1 = Upper class (Annual income > 20,000 rupees)
	A_2 = Lower class(Annual income $\leq$ 20,000 rupees)
B = Area\Location	B_1 = City (Town)
	B_2 = Rural
C = Sex	C_1 = Boys
	C_2 = Girl

- Dependent Variables

Degree of Self context Insecurity

HYPOTHESIS

Ho_1 : There is no significant difference between Means(M) of the degree of Self context Insecurity between Upper and lower class youth.

Ho_2 : There is no significant difference between Means(M) of the degree of Self context Insecurity between city and rural area youth.

Ho_3 : There is no significant difference between Means(M) of the degree of Self context Insecurity between boys and girls.

TOOLS

- Personal information sheet
- Insecurity measurement scale (Dr. Beena Shah)
- Statistical analysis of data by F-Anova test using 2x2x2 factorial design

SAMPLE

Total 240 youngsters were selected. Out of 240, 120 were of Upper class and 120 were of lowerclass. Out of these 120, 60 were from city/town area and 60 were from rural area. Sex ratio was maintained 1:1 in this sample of 60. It means out of these 60, 30 were boys and 30 were girls.

STATISTICAL ANALYSIS

(Parekh and Dixit, 1995)

Table -1

Summary of the 2x2x2 analysis of variance based on degree of Self context Insecurity with respect to three independent variables

Score of Variable	Sum of Square	DF	Mean of Square	F	Sig.
Status (A)	357.70	1	357.70	25.88	0.01
Aria (B)	10.004	1	10.004	7.24	0.01
Sex (C)	85.20	1	85.20	6.77	0.05
A x B	1.20	1	1.20	0.87	N.S.
B x C	55.10	1	55.10	3.98	N.S.
A x C	47.70	1	47.70	3.45	N.S.
A x B x C	23.43	1	23.43	1.69	N.S.

Table -2

Mean Scores and difference of Mean degree of Self context Insecurity with respect to three independent variables

Independent Variables		N	Mean(M)	Difference Of Mean
Status (A)	Upper	120	9.69	0.39
	Lower	120	10.06	
Aria (B)	City(Town)	120	11.09	2.44
	Rural	120	8.65	
Sex (C)	Boys	120	9.28	1.19
	Girls	120	10.47	

RESULTS AND DISCUSSION

Ho_1 : There is no significant difference between Means(M) of the degree of Self context Insecurity between Upper and lower class youth.

The 'F – Value' for first set of independent variable was found 2.57 as shown in table-1. This result has 0.01 significance value. So above said hypothesis **Ho_1** cannot be accepted because result has significant difference. Thus statistical data of table-1 clearly shown that there is significant difference in the degrees of Self context Insecurity between Upper and lower class youth. Mean values for Upper and lower class were 9.87 and 10.06 respectively (Table-2). These mean values concluded that the degree of Self context Insecurity is significantly higher in lower class than that in higher class youth.

Ho$_2$: There is no significant difference between Means(M) of the degree of Self context Insecurity between city and rural area youth.

The 'F – Value' for second set of independent variable was found 2.51 as shown in table-1. This result has 0.01 significance value. So above said hypothesis **Ho$_2$** cannot be accepted because result has significant difference. Thus statistical data of table-1 clearly shown that there is significant difference in the degrees of Self context Insecurity between city and rural area youth. Mean values for city and rural area were 11.09 and 8.05 respectively (Table-2). These mean values concluded that the degree of Self context Insecurity is significantly higher in city area than that rural area youth.

Ho$_3$: There is no significant difference between Means(M) of the degree of Self context Insecurity between boys and girls.

The 'F – Value' for first independent variable was found 3.31 as shown in table-1. This result has 0.05 significance value. So above said hypothesis **Ho$_3$** cannot be accepted because result has significant difference. Thus statistical data of table-1 clearly shown that there is significant difference in the degrees of Self context Insecurity between boys and girls. Mean values for Upper and lower class were 9.28 and 10.97 respectively (Table-2). These mean values concluded that the degree of Self context Insecurity is significantly higher in girls that that in boys.

CONCLUSION

Finally we can conclude this study in following three conclusions:

- Self context Insecurity is significantly higher in lower class than that of upper class.
- Self context Insecurity is significantly higher in city area than that rural area youth.
- Self context Insecurity is significantly higher in girls that that in boys.

VIII. PEER GROUP CONTEXT INSECURITY COMPARISON BETWEEN HIGHER AND LOWER CLASS YOUTH

Man interacts with man by many ways during his whole life and strikes with many hurdles while interacting with such biotic factors. He faces many state of his own mind. One of these state is Inferiority complex. When man does not get his basic requirements, he gradually develops Inferiority complex in his mind. And this Inferiority complex gradually develops in to 'Insecurity'. Insecurity means "The Inferiority complex created due to the external factors/catalysis of surrounding environment". Moreover Dr Sigmund Freund said that man suffered by inferiority complex with rather higher intensity in groups. Here we try to measure the degree of Peer Group-context Insecurity by taking three independent variables in account (Raja, 1982).

OBJECTIVES

- To measure degree of Peer Group context Insecurity in upper and lower class youth
- To compare degree of Peer Group context Insecurity between upper and lower class youth

RESEARCH METHODOLOGY : (Dhila, 2004; Shah, 1989)

- Independent Variables

A = Economical Status A_1 = Upper class (Annual income > 20,000 rupees)

A_2 = Lower class(Annual income $\leq$ 20,000 rupees)

B = Area\Location $\qquad$ B$_1$ = City (Town)

$\qquad\qquad\qquad\qquad$ B$_2$ = Rural

C = Sex $\qquad\qquad\qquad$ C$_1$ = Boys

$\qquad\qquad\qquad\qquad$ C$_2$ = Girl

- Dependent Variables

Degree of Peer Group context Insecurity

HYPOTHESIS

Ho$_1$: There is no significant difference between Means(M) of the degree of Peer Group context Insecurity between Upper and lower class youth.

Ho$_2$: There is no significant difference between Means(M) of the degree of Peer Group context Insecurity between city and rural area youth.

Ho$_3$: There is no significant difference between Means(M) of the degree of Peer Group context Insecurity between boys and girls.

TOOLS

- Personal information sheet
- Insecurity measurement scale (Dr. Beena Shah)
- Statistical analysis of data by F-Anova test using 2x2x2 factorial design

SAMPLE

Total 240 youngsters were selected. Out of 240, 120 were of Upper class and 120 were of lowerclass. Out of these 120, 60 were from city/town area and 60 were from rural area. Sex ratio was maintained 1:1 in this sample of 60. It means out of these 60, 30 were boys and 30 were girls.

STATISTICAL ANALYSIS:

(Parekh and Dixit, 1995)

Table -1

Summary of the 2x2x2 analysis of variance based on degree of Peer Group context Insecurity with respect to three independent variables

Score of Variable	Sum of Square	DF	Mean of Square	F	Sig.
Status (A)	611.204	1	1.204	11.29	0.01
Aria (B)	5.704	1	5.704	5.33	0.01
Sex (C)	49.504	1	49.504	4.62	N.S.
A x B	44.204	1	44.204	4.12	N.S.
B x C	27.334	1	27.339	2.55	N.S.
A x C	71.504	1	71.504	6.58	0.05
A x B x C	105.337	1	105.337	9.84	0.01

Table -2

Mean Scores and difference of Mean degree of Peer Group Peer Group Insecurity with respect to three independent variables

Independent Variables		N	Mean(M)	Difference Of Mean
Status (A)	Upper	120	12.18	3.2
	Lower	120	8.98	
Aria (B)	City(Town)	120	10.43	0.3
	Rural	120	10.73	
Sex (C)	Boys	120	10.73	6.9
	Girls	120	11.03	

RESULTS AND DISCUSSION

Ho_1 : There is no significant difference between Means(M) of the degree of Peer Group context Insecurity between Upper and lower class youth.

The 'F – Value' for first set of independent variables were shown in table-1. This result has 0.01 significance value. So above said hypothesis Ho_1 cannot be accepted because result has significant difference. Thus statistical data of table-1 clearly shown that there is significant difference in the degrees of Peer Group context Insecurity between Upper and lower class youth.

Ho$_2$: There is no significant difference between Means(M) of the degree of Peer Group context Insecurity between city and rural area youth.

The 'F – Value' for second set of independent variables were shown in table-1. This result has 0.01 significance value. So above said hypothesis **Ho$_2$** cannot be accepted because result has significant difference. Thus statistical data of table-1 clearly shown that there is significant difference in the degrees of Peer Group context Insecurity between city and rural area youth. Mean values for city and rural area were 11.09 and 8.05 respectively (Table-2). These mean values concluded that the degree of Peer Group context Insecurity is significantly higher in city area than that rural area youth.

Ho$_3$: There is no significant difference between Means(M) of the degree of Peer Group context Insecurity between boys and girls.

The 'F – Value' for first independent variables were shown in table-1. This result has no significance value. So above said hypothesis **Ho$_3$** can be accepted because result has significant difference. Thus statistical data of table-1 clearly shown that there is no significant difference in the degrees of Peer Group context Insecurity between boys and girls.

CONCLUSION

Finally we can conclude this study in following three conclusions:

- Peer Group context Insecurity is significantly higher in lower class than that of upper class.

- Peer Group context Insecurity is almost equal in city area than that rural area youth.
- Peer Group context Insecurity is insignificantly differ between girls and boys.

IX. SCHOOL CONTEXT INSECURITY
COMPARISON BETWEEN HIGHER AND LOWER CLASS YOUTH

When man does not get his basic requirements, he gradually develops Inferiority complex in his mind. And this Inferiority complex gradually develops in to 'Insecurity'. Insecurity means "The Inferiority complex created due to the external factors/catalysis of surrounding environment". Moreover Dr Sigmund Freund said that man suffered by inferiority complex with rather higher intensity in groups. Here we try to measure the degree of School-context Insecurity by taking three independent variables in account (Raja, 1982).

OBJECTIVES

- To measure degree of School context Insecurity in upper and lower class youth
- To compare degree of School context Insecurity between upper and lower class youth

RESEARCH METHODOLOGY

(Dhila, 2004; Shah, 1989)

- Independent Variables

A = Economical Status A_1 = Upper class (Annual income > 20,000 rupees)

A_2 = Lower class(Annual income $\leq$ 20,000 rupees)

46

B = Area\Location B_1 = City (Town)

B_2 = Rural

C = Sex C_1 = Boys

C_2 = Girl

- Dependent Variables

Degree of School context Insecurity

HYPOTHESIS

Ho_1 : There is no significant difference between Means(M) of the degree of School context Insecurity between Upper and lower class youth.

Ho_2 : There is no significant difference between Means(M) of the degree of School context Insecurity between city and rural area youth.

Ho_3 : There is no significant difference between Means(M) of the degree of School context Insecurity between boys and girls.

TOOLS

- Personal information sheet
- Insecurity measurement scale (Dr. Beena Shah)
- Statistical analysis of data by F-Anova test using 2x2x2 factorial design

SAMPLE

Total 240 youngsters were selected. Out of 240, 120 were of Upper class and 120 were of lowerclass. Out of these 120, 60 were from city/town area and 60 were from rural area. Sex ratio was maintained 1:1 in these sample of 60. It means out of these 60, 30 were boys and 30 were girls.

STATISTICAL ANALYSIS:

(Parekh and Dixit, 1995)

Table -1

Summary of the 2x2x2 analysis of variance based on degree of School context Insecurity with respect to three independent variables

Score of Variable	Sum of Square	DF	Mean of Square	F	Sig.
Status (A)	519.204	1	519.204	29.72	0.01
Aria (B)	5.104	1	5.104	2.92	N.S.
Sex (C)	40.838	1	40.838	2.32	0.05
A x B	47.704	1	47.704	2.73	N.S.
B x C	92.504	1	92.504	5.29	0.05
A x C	139.588	1	139.588	7.99	0.05
A x B x C	49.504	1	49.504	2.89	N.S.

Table -2

Mean Scores and difference of Mean degree of School context Insecurity with respect to three independent variables

Independent Variables		N	Mean(M)	Difference Of Mean
Status (A)	Upper	120	10.65	2.94
	Lower	120	7.71	
Aria (B)	City(Town)	120	9.03	0.3
	Rural	120	9.33	
Sex (C)	Boys	120	8.77	0.82
	Girls	120	9.59	

Results and Discussion:

Ho$_1$: There is no significant difference between Means(M) of the degree of School context Insecurity between Upper and lower class youth.

The 'F – Value' for first set of independent variable was found 2.94 as shown in table-1. This result has 0.01 significance value. So above said hypothesis **Ho$_1$** cannot be accepted because result has significant difference. Thus statistical data of table-1 clearly shown that there is significant difference in the degrees of School context Insecurity between Upper and lower class youth. Mean values for Upper and lower class were 9.87 and 10.06 respectively (Table-2). These mean values concluded that the degree of School context Insecurity is significantly higher in lower class than that in higher class youth.

49

Ho$_2$: There is no significant difference between Means(M) of the degree of School context Insecurity between city and rural area youth.

The 'F – Value' for second set of independent variable was found 0.31 as shown in table-1. This result has 0.01 significance value. So above said hypothesis **Ho$_2$** can be accepted because result has significant difference. Thus statistical data of table-1 clearly shown that there is no significant difference in the degrees of School context Insecurity between city and rural area youth.

Ho$_3$: There is no significant difference between Means(M) of the degree of School context Insecurity between boys and girls.

The 'F – Value' for first independent variable was found 0.82 as shown in table-1. This result has 0.05 significance value. So above said hypothesis **Ho$_3$** cannot be accepted because result has significant difference. Thus statistical data of table-1 clearly shown that there is significant difference in the degrees of School context Insecurity between boys and girls. Mean values for Upper and lower class were 9.28 and 10.97 respectively (Table-2). These mean values concluded that the degree of School context Insecurity is significantly higher in girls that that in boys.

CONCLUSION

Finally we can conclude this study in following three conclusions:

- School context Insecurity is significantly higher in lower class than that of upper class.
- School context Insecurity is insignificantly differ between city and rural area youth.
- School context Insecurity is significantly higher in girls that that in boys.

X. EXAM CONTEXT INSECURITY
COMPARISON BETWEEN HIGHER AND LOWER CLASS YOUTH

When man does not get his basic requirements, he gradually develops Inferiority complex in his mind. And this Inferiority complex gradually develops in to 'Insecurity'. Insecurity means "The Inferiority complex created due to the external factors/catalysis of surrounding environment". Here we try to measure the degree of Exam-context Insecurity by taking three independent variables in account (Raja, 1982).

OBJECTIVES

- To measure degree of Exam context Insecurity in upper and lower class youth
- To compare degree of Exam context Insecurity between upper and lower class youth

RESEARCH METHODOLOGY

(Dhila, 2004; Shah, 1989)

- Independent Variables

A = Economical Status A_1 = Upper class (Annual income > 20,000 rupees)

A_2 = Lower class(Annual income ≤ 20,000 rupees)

B = Area\Location B_1 = City (Town)

                           B_2 = Rural

C = Sex C_1 = Boys

                           C_2 = Girl

- Dependent Variables

Degree of Exam context Insecurity

HYPOTHESIS

Ho_1 : There is no significant difference between Means(M) of the degree of Exam context Insecurity between Upper and lower class youth.

Ho_2 : There is no significant difference between Means(M) of the degree of Exam context Insecurity between city and rural area youth.

Ho_3 : There is no significant difference between Means(M) of the degree of Exam context Insecurity between boys and girls.

TOOLS

- Personal information sheet
- Insecurity measurement scale (Dr. Beena Shah)
- Statistical analysis of data by F-Anova test using 2x2x2 factorial design

SAMPLE

Total 240 youngsters were selected. Out of 240, 120 were of Upper class and 120 were of lowerclass. Out of these 120, 60 were from city/town area and 60 were from rural area. Sex ratio was maintained 1:1 in these sample of 60. It means out of these 60, 30 were boys and 30 were girls.

STATISTICAL ANALYSIS

(Parekh and Dixit, 1995)

Table -1

Summary of the 2x2x2 analysis of variance based on degree of Exam context Insecurity with respect to three independent variables

Score of Variable	Sum of Square	DF	Mean of Square	F	Sig.
Status (A)	1.383	1	1.383	3.29	0.05
Aria (B)	45.937	1	45.937	8.21	0.05
Sex (C)	8.438	1	8.438	1.51	0.05
A x B	5.338	1	5.338	1.35	N.S.
B x C	10.004	1	10.004	1.79	N.S.
A x C	9.204	1	9.204	1.65	N.S.
A x B x C	51.337	1	51.337	9.19	0.05

Table -2

Mean Scores and difference of Mean degree of Exam Exam Insecurity with respect to three independent variables

Independent Variables		N	Mean(M)	Difference Of Mean
Status (A)	Upper	120	3.11	0.17
	Lower	120	3.28	
Aria (B)	City(Town)	120	2.76	0.87
	Rural	120	3.63	
Sex (C)	Boys	120	3.00	0.38
	Girls	120	3.38	

RESULTS AND DISCUSSION

Ho_1 : There is no significant difference between Means(M) of the degree of Exam context Insecurity between Upper and lower class youth.

The 'F – Value' for first set of independent variables were in table-1. This result has 0.05 significance value. So above said hypothesis Ho_1 cannot be accepted because result has significant difference. Thus statistical data of table-1 clearly shown that there is significant difference in the degrees of Exam context Insecurity between Upper and lower class youth. Mean values for Upper and lower class were 9.87 and 10.06 respectively (Table-2). These mean values concluded that the degree of Exam context

Insecurity is significantly higher in lower class than that in higher class youth.

Ho$_2$: There is no significant difference between Means(M) of the degree of Exam context Insecurity between city and rural area youth.

The 'F – Value' for second set of independent variables were shown in table-1. This result has 0.05 significance value. So above said hypothesis **Ho$_2$** cannot be accepted because result has significant difference. Thus statistical data of table-1 clearly shown that there is significant difference in the degrees of Exam context Insecurity between city and rural area youth. Mean values for city and rural area were 11.09 and 8.05 respectively (Table-2). These mean values concluded that the degree of Exam context Insecurity is significantly higher in city area than that rural area youth.

Ho$_3$: There is no significant difference between Means(M) of the degree of Exam context Insecurity between boys and girls.

The 'F – Value' for first independent variables were shown in table-1. This result has 0.05 significance value. So above said hypothesis **Ho$_3$** cannot be accepted because result has significant difference. Thus statistical data of table-1 clearly shown that there is significant difference in the degrees of Exam context Insecurity between boys and girls. Mean values for Upper and lower class were 9.28 and 10.97 respectively (Table-2). These mean values concluded that the degree of Exam context Insecurity is significantly higher in girls that that in boys.

CONCLUSION

Finally we can conclude this study in following three conclusions:

- Exam context Insecurity is significantly higher in lower class than that of upper class.
- Exam context Insecurity is significantly higher in city area than that rural area youth.
- Exam context Insecurity is significantly higher in girls that that in boys.

XI. OVERCOMING INSECURITY AND LOW SELF ESTEEM

REAL SELF CONFIDENCE AND ESTEEM IS BASED IN EMOTION, NOT A SELF IMAGE

To build self confidence and overcome low self esteem is to change how we feel emotionally about ourselves. To change our emotion requires changing two different core beliefs about self image. The first core belief is obvious. It is the belief that we are not good enough. It may have a more specific association to how we look, how smart we are, money, or lack of confidence sexually. The second core belief to change is the image of success that we feel we should be. Changing this belief is contrary to logic, but is a must if we are to overcome insecurity and raise our self esteem.

FALSE SELF IMAGE OF PERFECTION CAUSE OF LOW SELF ESTEEM AND LACK OF CONFIDENCE

When your mind has an image of success that you "should be" it associates happy emotions with that picture. I call that the image of perfection in our mind. The mind does a comparison between the image of perfection and how you see your self image currently. The comparison results in judgment and self rejection for not meeting the image of perfection. The self rejection results in feeling unworthy and of low self esteem

While the image of perfection appears to be a way for us to feel good about ourselves, it is actually causing us to reject ourselves which creates feelings of "not being good enough." If you were to dissolve the belief that you should fit into the image of perfection you would eliminate the self rejection and feelings of unworthiness that result.

FEELINGS OF CONFIDENCE AND SECURITY MEANS NO SELF REJECTION.

The approach of dissolving our image of perfection sounds contrary to our sense of logic about building confidence and esteem. This is because we have the belief that achieving the image of perfection will result in positive happy emotions and feeling confident with our success. Our mind has actually been programmed to have these emotional associations. We desire to feel these feelings and chase the image of perfection we have attached to them.

What we may not be aware of is that achieving our image of success doesn't effectively change our emotional state. It doesn't do anything to permanently change the way the voice in our head speaks to us or what we believe about ourselves. Many times people have achieved their goals only to find themselves still unfulfilled. Your emotional state may briefly change in the euphoria if the immediate success. But the core belief of not being good enough and your long term habit of self rejection in the mind hasn't been altered. The critical voice in our head is more likely to put a higher goal in front of us to achieve. I was talking with a woman who competed on the US Olympic Ski team several years back. She described feeling like a failure because she was only ranked about 10th in the world. It's okay to have high goals, but you don't have to make your love and self acceptance dependent on them.

CHANGE WHAT YOU BELIEVE AND YOU CHANGE HOW YOU FEEL EMOTIONALLY

The second belief to dissolve is that we are inadequate and somehow not good enough. These are the beliefs that create emotions of insecurity and fear. The emotions are not the problem they are just the resulting symptom of negative core beliefs. The "not good enough" image is a construct of our imagination. It is a belief about ourselves created by the mind concluding that we are "not good enough to meet the image of perfection." A step to changing this belief is to recognize that we the one observing the "self" image. We can not be the "self" image we are looking at. We are the one doing the looking. This means the "self image we create is really a "non self" image. With awareness we can decide to believe in the "non self" image or not believe in the "non self" image. Having this awareness helps shift our point of view and is a beginning step that will help us change a belief.

Changing the "not good enough" image is much easier once you have broken your belief in the image of perfection. Without the image of perfection you no longer have the comparison reinforcing the unworthy "self" image.

YOU ARE NOT AN IMAGE IN YOUR MIND - YOU CREATE THEM

Lack of awareness about how your mind misleads you can result in failed efforts to improve your confidence, and self esteem. Often people try to prop up their confidence with efforts to become their image of perfection. This great effort usually involves reinforcing the belief that we should be that fictional image. The result is a stronger mechanism for self rejection. With awareness we can avoid chasing these false beliefs and spend our time on what really makes a difference in the way we feel.

Real change in how you feel emotionally begins with becoming aware of the beliefs and thoughts in the mind. The second step is to change those core beliefs. Self Mastery Audio Sessions provide focused exercises to identify and change core beliefs. This in turn changes how you feel about your self. The first four audio coaching sessions are available for free.

If you can begin to change some of the smaller thoughts and emotions you have, then you can learn how to change the larger thoughts and emotions you experience. The next step is to sign up and listen and practice the Self Mastery Exercises.

REFERENCES

Raja B., (April-1982). A comparative study of the feelings of insecurity and degree of purpose in life among the aurally hendicapped and non-handicapped males and females, A dissertation Report - Guide Dr. I.D. Bhatt, Baroda.

Patel S.N., (2013). A comparative study of 'Insecurity' in higher and lower class youth. ACME International Journal of multidisciplinary Research. Vol. 1, Issue: 7, Page-23

Shah A.G., (1989). Research Methodology, 3rd edition, Anada publication, Ahemdabad.

Dhila B.D., (2004). Research Methodology, M.S. Shah mahila arts college, Kadi, North Gujarat.

Patel S.N., (2013). A comparative study of 'Study context Insecurity' in upper and lower class youth. Gujarat Manovigyan Darshan – Journal of Psychology and Education. Vol. 12, Issue: 16, Page-59.

Parekh A.C., Dixit S.K., (1995). Statistical analysis in psychological research, Champa publication, Junagadh.

Patel S.N., (2013). A comparative study of 'Survival contex Insecurity' in upper and lower class youth. PERIPEX – Indian Journal of Research. Vol. 2, Issue: 6, Page-23.

Patel S.N., (2013). A comparative study of 'Family contex Insecurity' in upper and lower class youth. PERIPEX – Indian Journal of Research. Vol. 2, Issue: 6, Page-23..

Patel S.N., (2013). A comparative study of 'Self-contex Insecurity' in upper and lower class youth. Global Research Analysis. Vol. 2, Issue: 10, Page-28.